Enlightenment

Lottie Dixon

BookLeaf Publishing

India | USA | UK

Presentation by *BookLeaf Publishing*

Web: www.bookleafpub.com

E-mail: info@bookleafpub.com

ISBN: 978-93-5744-336-4

First edition 2023

DEDICATION

To my readers, may this inspire, challenge, and educate you.

To Demar and Anthony, thank you for helping decide my true love.

To my Memaw, Mom, Dad, and Brother; I finally did it!

ACKNOWLEDGEMENT

I want to thank those who did believe in my writing and believed in myself more than I ever have. There is a long list, but the very few I know outside my mother who saw my talent at an early age. I want to thank Demar Lillard, although we don't speak anymore; you showed me what an artist can feel from my words and painted it onto a canvas for myself and the world to see. Anthony Saavedra, I owe you everything for truly making me see what I am capable of. You're my best friend and I hope someday I too will see your poetry as well. I do wish you both well and hope you both are doing well. Thank you for everything!

Breathing World

Ylg is among one of the streams flowing from Hvergelmer.

Goin was a serpent under Ygdrasil.

Glaser, a grove in Asgard.

Delling was the daybreak.

Ratatosk, a squirrel in Ygdrasil.

Audhumbla was the cow that nourished the giant Ymer.

Sahrimner, the boar, the gods, and the heroes of Valhal live on.

Iva, a river in Jotunheim.

Lerad, a tree near Valhal.

Legacy

Something not of Gold or Silver
Not Jeweled or Cashmere either
It doesn't have to be inherited or given

I feel like it could genuinely only be built by you
for you
Knowledge is power, I believe
Much more value than money could ever buy

My legacy would be priceless
Much shared knowledge and life experience
A given chance to avoid those almost inevitable
mistakes
I want those to take my struggles
Learn from them, not endure them
Reflect and relate, but not dismiss or retaliate
I wanted better for those after me and as much
as before me
Those that had enduring moments from before
me weren't spent in vain
Just as myself,
those before me I mended their humanity, hope,
and faith within others

With every single goal achieved, a bruise fades,
a cut closes, and tears have dried

My legacy is simple
It is for me to be those before me, their closure
And for me to be their inspiration, to those after
me

What is Ideal

If I woke up and decided that money wasn't a
thing
Maybe told everyone money would remain the
same currency for anything you did for work
What if all jobs paid the same
What would you do
What would I do

I would travel
I would soak into all the history from above my
head to toe
Breath in the same air where my ancestors
fought for their freedom
I would educate and spread knowledge all over
this world
I would create picture perfect memories and
imagery as I soak in the wonders that surround
me
I would truly embrace what it truly means to be
free

Free of self-hate
Free of slaving the man
Free of creative limitations
Free to truly be me

That is what is ideal

Her

She sat there on the damp porch step in the
sorrowful cold rain, thinking to herself while she
ran her pale fingers through her hair, upon losing
her color, after hearing the words from his
soft-spoken lips.

How he just wanted to part ways and jump into a
truck going down that long, lonely dirt road.
But, it's what he called home.
Always have in his eyes, but that ride didn't have
to be in silence.
It didn't have to be lonely. He didn't have to run.
He did what he always could, what only he
knew to do.

I am scared and panicked about what might have
been there?
But, why?
Was she the blame, or was his own foolish
choices the blame of his discouragement?

No one may ever know. But, as she looked up at
the sky, she placed her pale hands over her head.
She sat a moment in silence and once began

chanting. Choking on her tears and reciting these lines,

"Not everything has to end badly."

To softly the blow is to let go. Let none bad shall pass; only the goodwill remains to last.
Clear your thoughts of the wicked waters, allow the blazing ray to dry up the sickness that once plagued your mind.
Just allow the past to be left behind.
Walk forward, not back, for that don't forget the start and the finish, for everyone has a dream or goal.

To achieve or be left untouched is their own choice, but for that.
Know your path, know your goals, ambitions, truths for all that is dear to you.
She was slowly lowering her hands down by her sides.
Drawing in the cold, damped air of the outside and she fell to her knees in the massive flood of her sorrows.
Only she could say or even think was...
"If only you knew..."

The Dear John Letter

Dear John,

I can't do this anymore
I doubt you would understand the grief and pain
you did put me in
I am writing this as a last attempt to let you in
See what has been bothering me day today
I see how you sway me to think the other way
How I am an issue
How I am a burden to you
How I am lucky to have someone,
like you

Well, I give up
I retire from making you happy
I will not continue to break things within myself
to restore things you lack within yourself
They said writing a "Dear John" letter is a
cowardly way out
I say it is my way of having you meet my terms
of endearment

I can't have you influence what I know makes
me happy
So I wrote this

I can't have you tell me you deserve for me to
hear you out
So I wrote this
I can't have you attempt to embrace me to hold
me back
So I wrote this
I can't have you pull me back into this
So I wrote this

I wrote this as my independence letter,
"Freedom"
My Dear John letter,
I am taking back my power,
I am putting up boundaries,
I am practicing self-love,

So, John-
This is my final goodbye,
I will allow this to be a memory you can reread,
learn from it and grow from it

Love,

"Your So-Called Everything"

Reality Check

The wants and needs of my mindset are fantasy
to reality
Desires driving by determination
I stand up, I exhale, to look back in the mirror
I can't help to feel invisible
Will power the efforts go unnoticed?
Am I the one to blame?
How was I the one not told it mattered where I
placed my spotlight, where I placed and invested
my time into
Foolish me, life isn't refunded
But, I don't have to pay this toll to stay in the
arena I am currently
No matter what, we are always nomads
Moving ideas and ways of life from generation
to generation
Or the movement from the environment to better
ourselves as whole
Just like my ancestors, moving is for survival
Always better ways of resources to better
oneself
I think it's the thrill of the chase
Always chasing life
Moving as life passes around you, running after
the goals your desire

Just as you chase the clear skies in your sight as
the storm attempts to shackle your ankles
The screams of such struggle echo the air, but
the key seems non-existent
To unlock oneself is to find our true self
The key is positivity, which unlocks all doors of
your dreams to reality

Fear

I fear being unsuccessful the most
I also fear being a second choice and or alone
I fear the thoughts or doubts within me become a
reality to me
I fear losing the one I love the most
I fear feeling regret
But, above all, I fear not living by my own
standards

Fear can be positive or negative
Fear is a choice
The choice to embrace, conquer, or even drown
from it
Can fear be mistaken as to humble?
A healthy reminder of how I don't want my life
to be or go back to
Or am I overcompensating for not ever being
enough

Fear is a much deeper emotion than what we see
on the surface
Fear can be the root of many more emotions
Positive or Negative
I guess, it can be asked-
Can you be scared straight?

The Misunderstanding

I didn't tell you how much I needed you
I didn't tell you how much I had loved you
I didn't tell you how much you meant to me

I didn't think it would hurt this much
I didn't think I would lose you
I didn't think that I would have found someone I
would truly love

I have loved and lost before
I have given up on that idea of the perfect person
I have had no hope or faith for years and thought
of years to come

You came became the first for things
Showing your creative side,
Showing your emotional side,
Showing your heart and mind to me,

I apologize I didn't take better care of you
I apologize I didn't tell you my feelings
I apologize I didn't kiss you would I should have

Even then you had my attention,
and more so now you have my attention

My misunderstanding was I didn't think I could
fall in love with someone again
I misunderstood myself,
I underestimated the feelings I have for you

Happiness

To be happy for me is to know I have everything
I could ever want

Happiness could be as small as breathing the
fresh air from a mountain top
Or seeing the seedling, you planted sprout
Holding your child for the first time
Or watching your animals interact with other
wildlife

Happiness could be getting through those
college finals
Or obtaining that dream job, you always wanted
Seeing a company or someone take an interest in
your hobby or craft to make it a career
Or even starting your own business or helping
small businesses

Happiness could be a self-love journey
Or you start eating healthier
Setting boundaries for your family, friends,
peers, and others
Or getting hobbies that make you feel your inner
child again

Life is happiness
Growth is happiness
Self-love is happiness

Home

A house is not a home
A home is not a house
So, what do you call home?

As told before, your body is your temple
What if your lifestyle was your home?
Or is home the way you live your life?
I believe what home is, is that being comfortable
with yourself

Home to me is being present in life
To be yourself outside your "house"
Heard of "bringing drama home?"
The trick is not to allow it to get to you
Home is you
You are your home

Your mind is your safe space
Your body is your expression or what to decor
Your voice is that music you would blast or tv
show you would hear
Your senses are the bridge to familiarity

You're always home
Know yourself and your worth

Sell-Out

Do you have a price?
They always said someone has a price.
Is it money, gold, or true love?
What would you give up having it or obtain it
all?
If you succeed, can I ask you, will you stand
tall?

Would you rat out your brother or sister to
obtain their rank or status?
Would you twist the truth to have your way?
Would you give up your child?

If you had it all,
how much would that all be worth it?
Priced by pain and known you're the cause of it?
Sell-Out.

Sold what your life could have been?
Sold the life experiences?
Sold the life lessons, wisdom, relationships?
Could your price be worth all the simple things
in life?
How would you become a sell-out?

Maybe

My dreams, goals, and ambitions

The very thought of all I that I am wishing

The need and want to succeed

But not having you makes it hard to breathe

I have always been overjoyed for such success

Even if my life always became a mess

But, I thought I couldn't want anyone so badly

To haunt my thoughts daily

Always hear myself saying the phrase, "Just
Maybe.."

You're driving me crazy

The goals to own and be successful at
everything I do

It wouldn't mean a lot if I couldn't spend it with
someone like you

When I look at you, I see a man

With a huge plan to make such a huge impact on
this world

That is something I always adore

Every time I hear you speak, preach your ideas

I hung from every word

The twinkle of ambition in those stone brown
eyes

You're just simply one hell of a man

Humble, never forget where you came from

You know your self-worth, but have
understanding for others

I couldn't ask to have met anyone any better

Your gentle and kind-hearted, you don't reach
with one arm

But with opened arms

I look back into the mirror and around my
bedroom each day

How can someone who I adore and yearn for
this much

How can I keep such

But, every day, there is a phase as such, "Just
Maybe."

Faint

He was trapped in an eternal ice block
Unable to move to control his movements and
unwarp his mind
He was diagnosed with the frostbite that
attacked his heart
Numb to everything and all social interactions
Literally, the feeling of being alive but not living
was the true definition of his life

He was the chill that haunted the halls of his
peers
Cold dead stern stares straight from the void of
his heart of emptiness came from his slate pale,
hollow eyes he viewed the world with
He knew who he was; even the soft-spoken
heartfelt words or hugs of people whom he once
held close could spark a blitz to melt the icy
dungeon that enslaved his mind and heart

No one was ever genuine enough to him
Honesty was the cure, and this world had
abandoned it
To feel the loneliness in the comfort of his own
home shook his mind

To hear his own screams of help replay in his
mind but everyone's laughter drowned it out
He walks into a bathroom, locks the door, and
stares at his own icy reflection in the mirror
Shattered and raddled of the image he saw, the
void that engulfed him, and pounding his fist
into the mirror
The room painted into a crimson horror, and it
was the first time he had felt something
Looking down as his hands, picking the shards
of the busted mirror from his palms

A spirit of a girl had appeared.
She wore a yellow sundress covered with
flowers of Spring
Her hair was long and was the color of an
autumn shade of red, and she had hazel eyes and
a few freckles just over her cheeks
She had caressed his cheek and whispered,

"You're not alone. You have never been. What
you feel is merely hardships you endured.
Nothing lasts forever, and the pain could be
motivation. But, it needs direction. You can only
go up from here, and so you should be."

She held his hands, covering them as hers began
to burst into different shades of colors over his,
the blood becoming more faint and visible to see

She whispered, "Farewell, until we meet next
time."

Looking down at the shards that covered the
floor, he now saw color
The color was the shade of life

Us

They had dreams, goals and were full of
ambition
They dare to do the unthinkable
To journey to a land unimaginable
With Friend hand & hand
They were merely inseparable
My journey started 6 years ago
Just from a simple "Hello"
They grew and grew
They were each other's sunlight that shined
through
Sometimes, a stormy cloud may fog the
surroundings
The determination and trust
Fighting throughout the discouragement was a
must
For that, they weren't he or she
Me or I
But they were "Us"

A Warrior's Birthday

Nobles are good as their word
You're grown now, so you can see the world
Mother was gone too soon, but she did her best
To give you one hell of a fighting chance

You don't wear a crown
But a helm that you gained from your CClan
Symbolize you are their warlord

The finest silk hasn't ever touched your skin
But, you wear the pelts of your mother's armor

You walk with no guardsmen
You are partnered with your weapons, and you
forged from your own bare hands

No Kingdom you called home
But, the Clan's aged fort in the whispering forest

No huge feast was ever in your favor
But, the tavern you and your men attended, ale
was the greatest

You were not a Queen, nor a King
You lead your men into battles bravely
For that, you were a warrior

A Queen's Promise

She faces the people with such beauty and grace
Knowing choices, her king makes at hand
She places her reputation and image in his hands
Believing every word he has said until the very
end

Her people, she once said, looking into every
commoner and villager
She remembers twinkle in those children's eyes
How the lovely girls wish to be her
How the little boys wish to serve her
But, she knew the secrets of her king

The awful and unlawful things that made her
scream
The restless nights and looking at her throne
She wondered if she could do this on her own
One day the king's choice, confide in her
The day he since an innocent girl to die

That girl had to wish to be like the Queen
Something that convinces the Queen
Enough was enough

The dagger in the throne room was a prize in the
royal family
That night was the night the king was shown no
mercy as he banished the innocent girl to her
death

In the Queen's eyes to, she was banished
The innocence that lay within herself
The truth that was behind the crown itself

As the king was buried, at the resting, the Queen
rose up
And she spoke,
"I promise to be a better ruler over myself and to
my people. I may not be my king, but a leader is
1, not 2 or 3. I'm the ruler of my domain. Mine
only."

Worth

She is the most overlooked, always simply with
her nose in a book.
Shy and timid to her surroundings, she always
found herself away from the crowd.
She looks at him with curious eyes, and she can't
hide what lies within.
She sees the real troubles within, slowly
enduring the betrayal of the woman he is with.

The lies, fake smiles, and the unkept promises
from her to him.
He smiles, fights onto another day.
He sees the good within others.
Something he learned from his mother.
She begs and pleads, but he doesn't know how
much more he could endure.
Simply because he cares for her more.
As the shy girl watched from a distance, she
only wished he would stop to
listen.

To ask and hear her wisdom.
To guide him home, within himself.
To a man, pride is the most of him.
His image in his woman's eyes is key to him.

For the simple hot and cold behavior, to make
one question their own behavior.
To question your self-worth?
To question you as an issue?
Do they really care for you?

Know your worth, and know who is right for
you.
Her toxic lips are unhealthy for you.
But love is blind.
Love can kill.
But, most importantly...
Love is beautiful when in the form of
unconditionally and mutually.

Druid

She runs throughout terrain barefoot
The smallest wonders of the world caress her
feet
Her hair, if not wrapped around her face while
still
Her hair acts as a net to the leaves and flowers
around her

Winds spread her thoughts
Fire lights her way
Water cools her skin on a hot summer day
Earth summons familiars that will not lead her
astray

She dances within the rain
She roars with the thunder
She breathes life and summons new beginnings
to those around her

The animals adore her
The elements protect her
It is her that is their healer
She may not think she is powerful, but
remember

"Breaking stuff is easy and only two seconds,
but healing what is broken takes strength and
time. Healing is not easy."

10 Wonders

Bewitching feeling in Salem

Underwater of the reefs in Aruba

Cherry blossom tree leaves cover rivers in Japan

King Arthur's statue in Cornwall

Excitement to move to New Zealand

Thailand's kayaking journeys

Love for the valleys in Switzerland

Iceland's mountains with the aroura as the
Northern Lights

Safari exploring in Africa

Temple Petra in Jordan

Enlightenment

Enlightenment is the aftermath of the storm
The mental maelstrom
Conquering those thoughts, life challenges, to
evaluate to a higher being of yourself
Enlightenment doesn't come without pain or
suffering

Times of going without,
Times of living in doubt,
Times of not knowing what is about to happen
next?

Enlightenment is a superpower
Wisdom you have,
the power of knowing you can influence the
world
The power of knowing who you are
Your worth, limits, likes, or dislikes
Becoming superhuman

Those who or of what used to be harmful
You feel no pain
You feel remorse for them
You forgive easily
You let go of the past better
You are stronger

You peeked your enlightenment

The Author

Assuming your life is a story, and you're the
author, what does your happy ending look like?

An underdog hero?
Uncommon sidekick that turned hero?
Hero gone rogue?

A villain that carries the past and hate within
their heart?
Is there a redemption arc for you?
Or do you train a league?

Save children?
Have children?
Have a scaled or fur companion?

Fall in love with a Princess or Prince?
King or Queen?
A commoner?
Or a handsome Viking?

Did you make a difference?
Did you empower those around you?
Is there a statue of you?

Memories within the heart of those who
surrounded you?

Who are you in your book?
How will your story end?
Who did you save?
Who saved you?